BIOINDICATOR SPECIES

MONARCH BUTTERFLIES MATTER

by Cecilia Pinto McCarthy

Content Consultant
Christine Merlin, PhD
Assistant Professor, Department of Biology
Texas A&M University

Core Library
An Imprint of Abdo Publishing
abdopublishing.com

abdopublishing.com

Published by Abdo Publishing, a division of ABDO, PO Box 398166, Minneapolis, Minnesota 55439.

Printed in the United States of America, North Mankato, Minnesota
082015
012016

THIS BOOK CONTAINS RECYCLED MATERIALS

Cover Photo: Lisa Thornberg/iStockphoto
Interior Photos: Lisa Thornberg/iStockphoto, 1; iStockphoto, 4; Red Line Editorial, 6, 26; Rusty Dodson/Shutterstock Images, 9; Lowell Gordon/iStockphoto, 10; Frans Lanting/Mint Images/Newscom, 12; David Byron Keener/Shutterstock Images, 14, 43; Thomas Kitchin & Victoria Hurst/NHPA/Photoshot/Newscom, 16, 23; Nick James Stock/iStockphoto, 18; Shutterstock Images, 21; AP Images, 24; St. Petersburg Times/ZumaPress/Newscom, 28; Richard Ellis/ZumaPress/Newscom, 32; Brandon Pollock/Waterloo Courier/AP Images, 34; Mel Evans/AP Images, 36; John Dunham/Messenger-Inquirer/AP Images, 38, 45; Doug Strickland/Chattanooga Times Free Press/AP Images, 40

Editor: Jon Westmark
Series Designer: Laura Polzin

Library of Congress Control Number: 2015945399

Cataloging-in-Publication Data
McCarthy, Cecilia Pinto.
Monarch butterflies matter / Cecilia Pinto McCarthy.
p. cm. -- (Bioindicator species)
ISBN 978-1-68078-012-3 (lib. bdg.)
Includes bibliographical references and index.
1. Monarch butterflies--Juvenile literature. 2. Butterfly ecology--Juvenile literature. 3. Environmental protection--Juvenile literature. I. Title.
595.78--dc23

2015945399

CONTENTS

AN AMAZING JOURNEY

It is a sunny, late-August morning in northern Minnesota. A bright orange and black butterfly glides from flower to flower. It is a monarch butterfly searching for nectar to drink. The nectar will help give the butterfly energy to survive the coming winter. Soon the butterfly will join millions of other monarchs on an amazing journey. They will travel to Mexico,

Monarchs suck up nectar with their tongues, which act like straws.

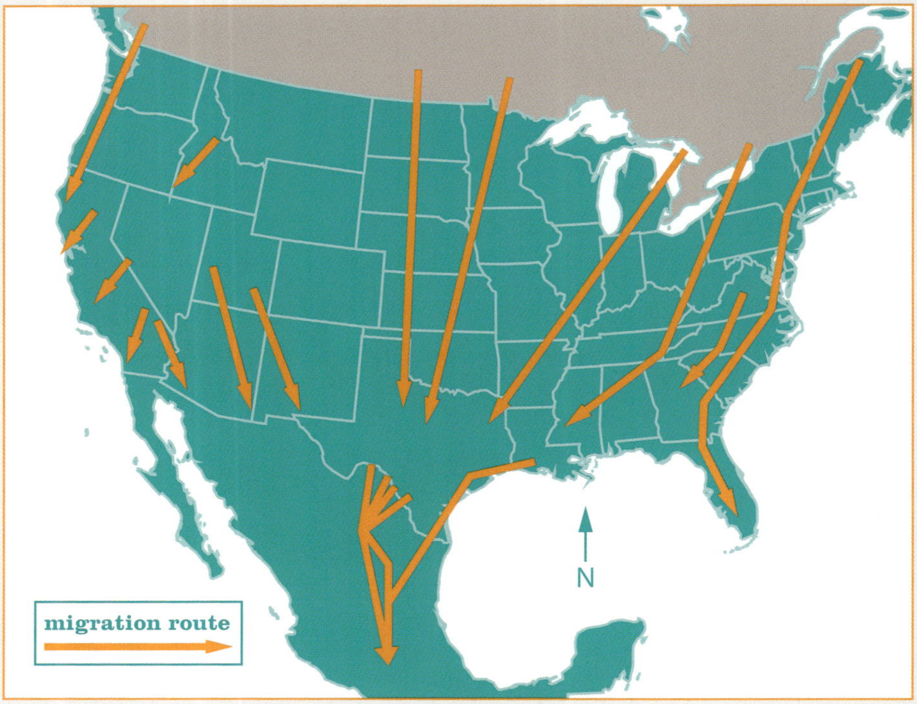

Migration Routes
The monarch butterfly has one of the longest known migrations of any insect. Over what parts of the United States do most of these butterflies fly? Why do you think different populations go to different areas?

almost 2,500 miles (4,230 km) away. In spring, new monarchs will return north.

In the central and eastern United States and Canada, the cooler, shorter days of fall signal to monarchs it is time to fly south. Monarchs cannot live through the North's harsh winters. Flowers cannot survive through cold winters, either. Monarchs depend on the nectar from flowers for survival. So the butterflies fly an average of 30 to 50 miles (48–75 km) each day in search of warmer weather. They rest at night, gathered in clusters. During the trip, the butterflies must avoid predators while finding food and shelter.

The monarchs have not made this journey before. They use signs from nature to find their way. On sunny days, the butterflies use the position of the sun to point themselves southward. When it is cloudy, they depend on special sensors. These sensors detect Earth's magnetic field. The monarchs can use the field to turn themselves in the right direction.

Becoming a Butterfly

A monarch begins life as a tiny egg stuck to the leaf of a milkweed plant. After approximately four days, the egg hatches into a green caterpillar. Now it must eat, eat, eat. The larva's first meal is its own egg case.

Then it feeds on the plant on which the egg grew. It eats nothing but leaves for the next two weeks.

As it grows, the caterpillar goes through five stages. Between each stage, the larva sheds its skin. It changes color. It becomes striped with yellow, white, and black bands. After 10 to 15 days, the larva can weigh up to 3,000 times its hatching weight.

When the caterpillar stops growing, it finds a safe place to hide. There it undergoes a change called metamorphosis. The larva spins a silk patch and attaches itself to a branch or other object. It hangs upside down and folds into a J shape. The larva sheds one last time. Now it is a green pupa, or chrysalis.

Approximately two weeks later, the pupa

Eating Milkweed

Once they leave their eggs, monarch caterpillars eat only milkweed. The monarchs get a special benefit from eating the plant. Milkweed leaves contain toxins that become stored in the caterpillar's body. The caterpillar and butterfly's bright colors warn other animals they are poisonous to eat.

Monarch caterpillars hang upside down and curl up before turning into pupas.

After approximately two weeks, monarchs break out of their pupas as butterflies.

splits open. A butterfly emerges. The butterfly weighs less than a small paper clip. Its wingspan is 3.5 to 4 inches (9–10 cm) wide.

The new butterfly has two tasks: mate and lay eggs. If it finds a partner, the butterfly can mate by the time it is eight days old. After mating, the female lays her eggs only on milkweed plants. It lays just one egg per plant. On average, a female lays between 300 and 400 eggs. So the butterfly must find hundreds of plants.

Making the Trip

A monarch's lifespan depends on the time of year it is born. Monarchs born in spring and summer live as adults for two to six weeks. But those born in late August and September are different. These butterflies do not mate right away. By not reproducing, they save energy for a long trip to Mexico.

Millions of monarchs travel from the eastern and central United States and Canada. They gather in Mexico's central mountains. This is their final

While wintering in Mexico, monarchs group together on branches and tree trunks.

destination. The cool, humid weather in the mountains is perfect for the butterflies. Nearby streams provide water for them to drink. Fir trees give them a safe place to roost.

Over the winter months, the butterflies live off the body fat they stored during their journey. The cool weather lowers the amount of energy the butterflies use. The butterflies crowd together until spring. By saving their energy, migrating monarchs can live for approximately eight months. Year after year, new generations of the butterflies return to the same roosting sites.

As spring approaches, roosting monarchs become more active. They begin to mate. By mid-March the butterflies begin the return trip north. The females seek out milkweed plants on the way in order to lay their eggs. As the butterflies die, new butterflies hatch and continue northward. It takes generations of butterflies to make the journey. They follow the growth of the milkweed northward. The

Scientists use monarch tags to track the butterflies' migration.

butterflies arrive in the northern United States and Canada by summer. They are the great- and great-great-grandchildren of the monarchs that spent the winter in Mexico.

Disappearing Monarchs

Scientists have tracked monarch migration since 1993. Each December people record the number of monarch colonies in Mexico. They also note how much land the groups occupy. Each acre holds approximately 25 million butterflies. Scientists use this number to figure out the total number of monarchs in the area.

In the late 1990s, scientists noticed that fewer of the butterflies were arriving in Mexico. Monarchs took up 45 acres (18 ha) of Mexican forest in the winter of 1996. The area dropped to 1.7 acres (0.67 ha) by 2013. That is a space just a little bigger than a football field. Scientists estimate the migrating population has shrunk by 90 percent over the past 20 years.

There are still millions of monarchs in North America. But this is far fewer than the more than one billion monarchs that migrated in the early to mid-1990s. Scientists are worried. Some think that with so few butterflies, the amazing migration may end.

PERSPECTIVES

Protecting Monarchs

Scientists filed a petition with the US Fish and Wildlife Service in August 2014. The petition asks that the monarch be declared as a threatened species. But some people who raise and sell butterflies are against the petition. It limits the number of monarchs that can be raised without a scientist to ten or fewer. The breeders worry this limit will hurt their businesses.

Monarchs are sensitive to changing weather conditions, such as varying amounts of rain and temperature changes.

Not Just For Looks

Monarchs are more than just beautiful insects. They are bioindicators. Bioindicators are plants and animals that are sensitive to changes in the world. They give people information about the health of the environment. Monarchs depend on plants throughout their lives. These butterflies are also sensitive to changes in temperature. A drop in the number of monarchs can be a sign that there are bigger problems in an ecosystem.

EXPLORE ONLINE

Chapter One discusses how some populations of monarchs travel to Mexico for the winter. Below is a link to a story written by a woman who found a monarch tag while visiting Mexico. Monarch tags are used to track the butterfly's movement. What information in the story is similar to the information in Chapter One?

The Monarch Tag That Traveled Round Trip

mycorelibrary.com/monarch-butterflies-matter

A CHANGING WORLD

Butterflies make great bioindicators because of their uncommon life cycle. At each stage, the butterfly has special needs. Changes in monarch populations give clues to bigger problems in the world. These problems not only affect butterflies but also other animals, plants, and humans.

Monarchs interact with the environment in different ways as caterpillars and butterflies.

Milkweed

A pollutant called ozone can damage milkweed leaves. Ozone is a gas. Ozone high in the atmosphere protects Earth from the sun's rays. But the gas can also form near Earth. The gas is created from heat and pollution. Ground-level ozone causes human health problems. It also hurts some plants. Ozone keeps milkweed from making food for itself. Milkweed damaged by ozone has small dark spots on its leaves.

The Pollution Problem

Monarchs cannot live without milkweed. They need it to lay their eggs. And it is their food source while they are caterpillars. But milkweed has disappeared along with monarchs.

At one time, there was much milkweed in the midwestern United States in the area known as the Corn Belt. Most of the country's corn and soy are grown in the Corn Belt. Milkweed levels started to go down when farmers began spraying their crops with herbicides. These chemicals can kill milkweed. Most migrating monarchs go through the Corn Belt. But today there is little milkweed in the region. The

Farmers and gardeners often spray chemicals to kill weeds and harmful insects.

number of Midwest monarchs dropped by 81 percent from 1999 to 2010. This drop may be a sign chemicals are hurting the ecosystem.

People spray chemicals on roadsides and gardens across the United States. Many other insects, including bees, also depend on flowering plants. Chemicals in the environment harm insects, frogs, toads, and other animals. These chemicals enter the

PERSPECTIVES

Corn for Cash

The US government's Conservation Reserve Program (CRP) pays farmers not to plant on environmentally important land. But many farmers struggle to earn a living. Chances to increase income are not easily passed up. In 2007 the US government ordered that ethanol be added to fuels. Ethanol is made from corn. Many farmers saw a chance to raise their income by planting more corn. Many Midwest farmers plowed more land to grow corn. Some used CRP land where milkweed and nectar plants grew. More than 7 million acres (2.8 million ha) of CRP land were lost.

food web when animals take them in. Once in the food web, the chemicals can harm people.

Lost Land

Open land throughout the United States is being used up. People are building more houses and businesses. Farmers are planting on more land so they can sell more crops. More than 6,000 acres (2,428 ha) of land in the United States are lost to development every day. Natural habitats filled with wildflowers and weeds were once common along highways, roadsides,

Mowing milkweed near roads destroys important monarch habitats.

ditches, and streams. But mowing in these areas is hurting habitats used by butterflies and other animals.

Habitat loss is also a problem in Mexico. In 1986 the Monarch Butterfly Biosphere Reserve was started to protect monarchs. But illegal logging in the area is reducing the number of trees where the butterflies can roost.

Fewer trees means less shelter from bad weather. Dry monarchs can survive temperatures as low as 24 degrees Fahrenheit (-4°C). Wet monarchs freeze to death at this temperature. Windy weather can also hurt monarchs by causing them to dry out. Cutting

Snowfall in western Mexico in January 1996 killed millions of wintering monarchs.

down trees has wiped out entire monarch colonies in some places.

Climate Change

The world's climate is changing. Some areas are facing higher temperatures or droughts. Others are seeing wetter conditions and more frequent severe weather. Monarchs are easily affected by extreme weather. In 2002 a winter storm in Mexico killed up to 270 million roosting butterflies.

Climate change also affects the plants monarchs eat. In 2011 record droughts and wildfires in Texas killed off much of the milkweed and flowers. Many caterpillars died from lack of food.

Climate change may also affect how monarchs migrate. Exactly how the butterflies will react is difficult to predict. Many things affect how and when monarchs travel. One component is milkweed growth. Milkweed does not grow in cold weather. But as temperatures rise, some types of milkweed will grow farther north in Canada. Monarchs migrating in spring follow milkweed as it starts to grow. If milkweed grows farther north, the butterfly's range may shift northward. This change would give monarchs a longer trip to their roosting sites in Mexico. A longer journey increases the chance the butterflies will die before reaching their destination.

Higher temperatures could hurt monarchs in other ways. Warm temperatures make butterflies more active. More lively butterflies use more energy. Extreme heat can kill butterflies. If temperatures rise enough, monarchs may stop migrating. Scientists have found that nonmigratory butterflies are more likely to get sick.

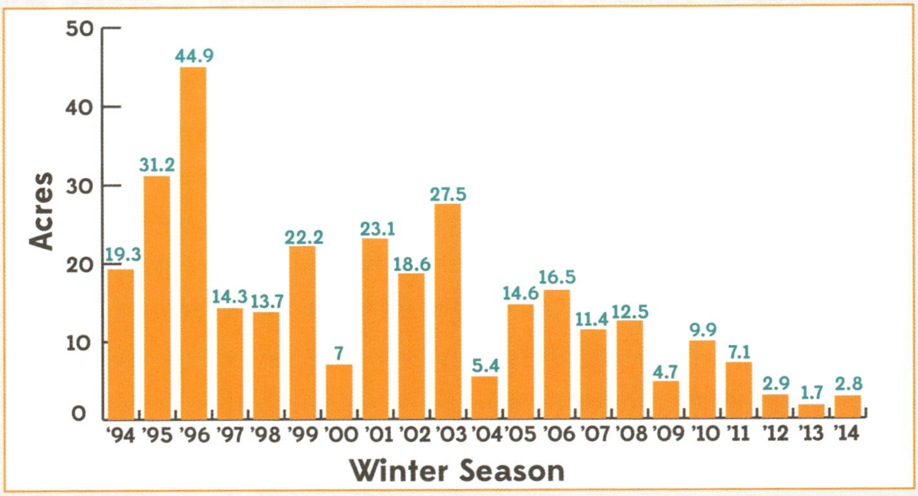

Roosting Monarchs

This graph shows the area taken up by monarchs wintering in Mexico from 1994 to 2014. Measuring the area taken up by these butterflies gives scientists an idea of how many migrating monarchs there are. How has the size of the roosting area changed over the years? What might be the causes for the yearly changes in population?

Scientists predict climate change in Mexico will bring higher temperatures and less rainfall. In 2009 a drought hit monarch roosting sites in Mexico. Fir trees, in which monarchs roost, are more prone to diseases and attacks by insects during droughts. Bark beetles attacked the trees. Mexican officials were forced to cut down several acres of forest. Shrinking forests threaten migrating monarchs' survival.

STRAIGHT TO THE SOURCE

Ecotourism is meant to bring nature and people together in a helpful way. But this is not always the case. Butterfly expert Lincoln Brower and environmentalist Homero Aridjis explain:

> *Ecotourism is presenting an additional threat to the butterflies as its popularity increases. As regular visitors to the monarch colonies, we have seen the conditions in these areas deteriorate, for butterflies and tourists. Along the heavily used trails that lead to the colonies . . . extensive areas of vegetation have been killed. Excessive dust, which now rises into the air with each step, is hazardous to the butterflies because it clogs their respiratory orifices. When we visited the Piedra Herrada site this February . . . a welcome sign on the trail leading to the butterflies read, "No more than 20 people in the Sanctuary." And yet we counted 24 tourist buses in the parking lot.*

Source: Lincoln P. Brower and Homero Aridjis. "The Winter of the Monarch," New York Times, The Opinion Pages, *March 15, 2013. Print.*

Point of View

The writers believe too much ecotourism is hurting the butterflies. What evidence do they give to support their point of view? What can be done to solve this problem?

CHAPTER THREE

MONARCHS MATTER

Seven US states have chosen the monarch as the state insect or butterfly. The butterfly's thousand-mile journey captures many people's imaginations. Every year thousands of schoolchildren learn about life cycles by watching monarchs go through changes in the classroom. But humans also benefit from these animals in less obvious ways.

Studying monarchs is a great way to learn more about how humans are connected to nature.

Monarchs in the Food Web

Monarch butterflies play a key role in the food web. A food web shows how plants and animals are connected to one another. Monarch caterpillars are an important source of food for some ants, wasps, and spiders. Some birds and spiders eat adult monarchs. Without monarchs these animals would need to find other sources of food. The loss of monarchs could upset the balance between predators and prey in an ecosystem.

Monarchs Pollinate Plants

Some plants use a substance called pollen to reproduce. Certain animals travel between flowers to find nectar to eat. When they touch the flowers, pollen sticks to their bodies. They then move the pollen to other flowers. This process is called pollination. Butterflies make good pollinators.

Pollinators help people grow crops. Insects, such as butterflies and bees, pollinate many of the world's food crops. These include fruits, vegetables, nuts, and spices. A drop in butterfly numbers can indicate issues affecting other pollinators, such as bees. Without pollinators, many of the fresh fruits and vegetables in grocery stores could disappear. These foods supply people with essential nutrients. Fewer fresh and healthy foods could mean worse nutrition for humans.

Much to Tell

As bioindicators, monarchs give the first glimpses into the problems caused by human actions. Studying monarchs can show us how entire ecosystems will be affected if climate change, habitat destruction, and harmful chemical use continue.

FURTHER EVIDENCE

Chapter Three covers some of the reasons why monarchs are important. Identify one reason why monarchs should be saved. Read the article at the website listed below. Does the article support the main point of Chapter Three? What new information does the website give?

Protecting Monarchs

mycorelibrary.com/monarch-butterflies-matter

CHAPTER FOUR

MAKING A DIFFERENCE

Migrating monarchs in North America depend on areas in Mexico, the United States, and Canada for survival. The three countries have formed a joint conservation plan. They are working together to save the butterflies. The main goal is to boost monarch populations by restoring and protecting butterfly habitats.

Monarchs flutter through the air in the Monarch Butterfly Biosphere Reserve in central Mexico.

Students in Iowa jump over tall prairie grass on their way to plant milkweed.

One of the hardest jobs people working to save monarchs have is changing the way people think about milkweed. Many people have grown up thinking of milkweed as a pest plant. More people are now learning the importance of these plants for butterflies and other insects. All over North America, people are planting milkweed and flowers for monarchs and other pollinators.

Three Nations United

The Mexican government created the Monarch Butterfly Biosphere Reserve in 1986. It includes the forests where many monarchs spend the winter. Before the reserve was created, farmers cut down trees for firewood and lumber. Now taking wood is illegal in the reserve. But some poor farmers continue to take and sell wood in order to support their families.

Organizations from the United States and Mexico are working together to find a solution. Groups are coming up with options to help farmers make a living

Growing flowering plants helps butterflies, bees, and other pollinators.

without hurting the important trees. Some of the locals now work in ecotourism. They guide tours to monarch colonies. Others are planting new forests that can provide wood to support their families.

Canada has declared three areas as Monarch Butterfly Reserves. These habitats contain grasses and wildflowers, making them perfect places for monarchs and other pollinators. The Canadian government has also listed monarchs as a species of special concern.

Groups in the United States are also working to protect butterfly habitats. Monarch Watch's Bring Back the Monarchs program aims to increase populations by planting milkweed and flowering plants throughout the United States. Monarch Watch volunteers also help scientists study butterfly populations by tagging monarchs.

In May 2015, the United States government published a national strategy to help

PERSPECTIVES

Phone App Trackers

Smartphone apps make it easy for anyone to report monarch sightings. The Journey North app allows people to record sightings of butterflies, birds, and much more. The University of Texas and Monarch Watch are making another app. This app is meant for people who are offshore in the Gulf of Mexico. They will be able to record monarch locations from boats and oil rigs. This information will help scientists understand how monarchs migrate in that area.

A student in Kentucky catches a butterfly during a monarch tagging event.

pollinators. The government plans to help pollinators by bringing back habitats and cutting back on harmful chemicals across the country. The strategy focuses on making a butterfly passage between Minnesota and Mexico. Milkweed and flowering plants will be planted alongside the highway. The goal is to raise the eastern population of monarchs from its winter 2014 estimated population of 56.5 million to 225 million by 2020.

Citizen Science

Ordinary people can learn about butterflies and help protect them. Anyone can be a citizen scientist by volunteering to collect information. Citizen scientists are important to helping butterflies. People of all ages collect data about monarchs and milkweed. Schoolchildren, gardeners, and other volunteers tag monarchs. Others gather milkweed samples. The data they collect is sent to professional scientists. The scientists use the data to learn what monarchs need.

Another way people across North America are helping monarchs is by making butterfly

Got Milkweed?

A Canadian group called the David Suzuki Foundation is working to sell milkweed seeds. It started the #gotmilkweed campaign in April 2014. Since then it has sold more than 4,000 milkweed plants in Toronto. People have planted the milkweed in parks and around schools.

Students in Tennessee plant bushes and other plants to attract butterflies.

way stations. A butterfly way station is a garden with milkweed plants and flowers where monarchs can eat and lay their eggs.

Bringing Change

Listening to monarchs' warnings is the first step toward helping save the monarch migration. The monarch's message can also increase people's awareness about chemical use and climate change. These issues do not only affect butterflies. They affect the health and survival of other insects, animals, and humans. In the end, everyone can benefit from listening to the message of the monarch butterfly.

STRAIGHT TO THE SOURCE

Monarchs are important to Mexican culture. Author Robert Pyle explains how the butterfly's migration became connected with the Mexican celebration of the Day of the Dead:

> *In Mexico, the Day of the Dead celebration on the first of November is celebrated with sugar skulls and marigolds . . . Another symbol of the spirit of the departed . . . is la monarca. A second name for monarchs in the villages near the winter clusters is las palomas, which means the doves, or the souls of lost children. When the monarchs come back in late fall, they are seen as the souls of those who died young, returning for their annual visit. I remember one . . . altar near the Diego Rivera museum. Thousands of real marigolds mingled with thousands more made of orange tissue paper and just as many monarchs made of crepe. . . .*

Source: Robert Michel Pyle. Chasing Monarchs. Migrating with the Butterflies of Passage. *New York: Houghton Mifflin Company, 1999. Print. 127.*

What's the Big Idea?

Read this passage carefully. What connection do monarch butterflies have with the Mexican celebration Day of the Dead? Do you think that the arrival of monarchs is a happy or sad experience for the Mexican people? How might the loss of returning monarchs affect Day of the Dead celebrations?

FAST FACTS

Common Name: Monarch butterfly

Scientific Name: *Danaus plexippus*

Average Wingspan: 3.5 to 4 inches (9–10 cm)

Average Weight: 0.0095 to 0.026 ounces (0.27–0.75 g)

Color: Orange with black lines and white spots. Black veins are thicker on the females' wings.

Average Life Span: Two to six weeks for butterflies born in spring and summer, and six to eight months for migrating butterflies

Diet: Milkweed leaves; nectar and water

Habitat: Warm regions where milkweed grows; fir, pine, oak, and cedar forests during winter

Predators: Birds, insects, spiders, parasites

What's Happening: The population of migrating monarch butterflies has declined.

Where It's Happening: North America

Why It's Happening: Climate change, habitat destruction, and pollution are hurting migration.

Why It's Important: Monarchs are bioindicators. Population decline warns of larger problems in the environment related to global warming, habitat destruction, and pollution.

What You Can Do

- Plant monarch way stations with milkweed and native flowering plants.
- Grow organically—do not use pesticides or herbicides.
- Join citizen science projects to help scientists.

STOP AND THINK

Another View

Chapter Two discusses how poor farmers in Mexico's Monarch Butterfly Biosphere Reserve sometimes cut down trees in order to make a living. Find another source that talks about the conflict between farmers and conservationists. Write a short essay comparing and contrasting the point of view of the farmer and conservationist.

You Are There

This book talks about how millions of monarchs migrate to Mexico. Imagine you are in the forest when the monarchs arrive. Write a letter home telling your friends what your experience is like. What do you notice about the forest, the mountains, and monarchs? Be sure to use plenty of details in your letter.

Tell the Tale

Chapter Four discusses how regular people are helping monarch butterflies by participating in citizen science projects. Imagine you are getting kids at your school involved in helping monarchs. Write a short speech encouraging your classmates to become citizen scientists. What would you plan to do to help monarchs?

Surprise Me

Chapter One describes the life cycle of the monarch. Choose two or three facts about monarchs that surprised you. Write a few sentences about each fact and why you were surprised.

GLOSSARY

ecotourism
travel to threatened areas in order to contribute to their protection

generation
a group of individuals born and living at the same time

herbicide
a chemical used to stop or kill plant growth

larva
a young form of an insect or other animal

metamorphosis
a change some species go through to become adults

migrate
to move from one place to another

nectar
sugary fluid contained in plants

pollinate
to transfer pollen between flowers

pupa
a stage of an insect before it becomes an adult

LEARN MORE

Books

Carney, Elizabeth. *Great Migrations: Whales, Wildebeests, Butterflies, Elephants, and Other Amazing Animals on the Move*. Washington, DC: National Geographic, 2010.

Lasky, Kathryn. *Monarchs*. Great Neck, NY: StarWalk Kids Media, 2014.

Rice, Dona Herweck. *Pollination*. Huntington Beach, CA: Teacher Created Materials, 2015.

Websites

To learn more about Bioindicator Species visit **booklinks.abdopublishing.com**. These links are routinely monitored and updated to provide the most current information available.

Visit **mycorelibrary.com** for free additional tools for teachers and students.

INDEX

ABOUT THE AUTHOR

Cecilia Pinto McCarthy writes about science and nature and teaches classes at a nature sanctuary. McCarthy enjoys hiking, photography, and playing the violin. She and her family live north of Boston, Massachusetts.